D1577827

MY FIRST
ANIMAL
COLORING
BOOK

ILLUSTRATED BY

Stacie Bloomfield

Find Stacie at www.gingiber.com | @gingiber on Instagram!

EMAIL US AT

modernkidpress@gmail.com

TO GET FREE GOODIES!

Just title the email "Amazing Animals!"
And we'll send you some extra worksheets
for your kiddo!!

Find us on Instagram!
@modernkidpress

this book belongs to:

_____

. . . .

_____

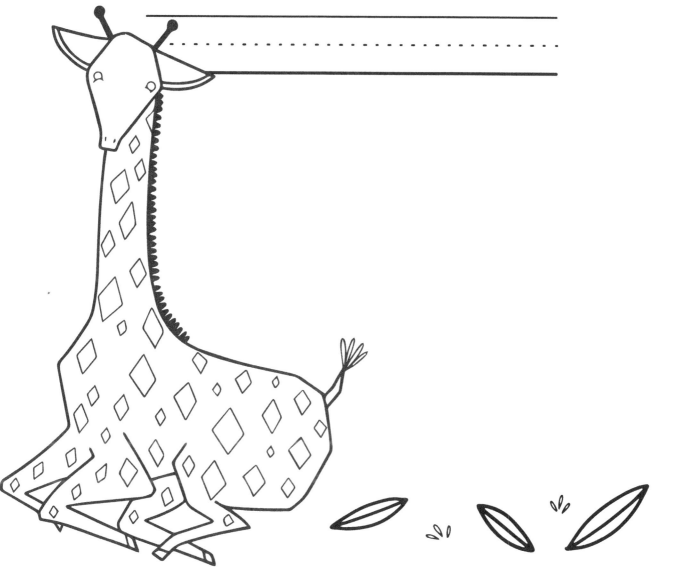

deer

Write the animal name below. Use your very best handwriting!

deer

deer

Scientific name: Cervidae

I can: run up to 30 mph

I eat: plants, twigs, fruits, nuts, and grass

I can live up to: 25 years

Fun fact: Deer can leap almost 8 feet high!

Can YOU jump 8 feet high?! Try and see!

sloth

Write the animal name below. Use your very best handwriting!

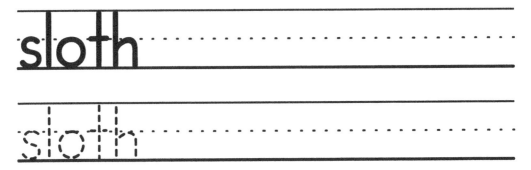

Scientific name: Folivora

I live: in rainforests around South & Central America

I eat: fruits, leaves, lizards and insects

I can live up to: 30 years old

Fun fact: Sloths are so slow they usually only move 1 foot every minute!

Do you like to go **sloooooow** or **fast**?!

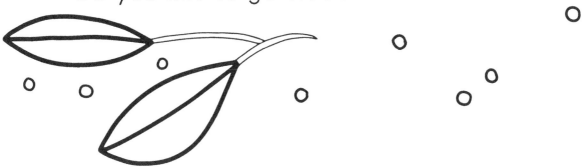

otter

Write the animal name below. Use your very best handwriting!

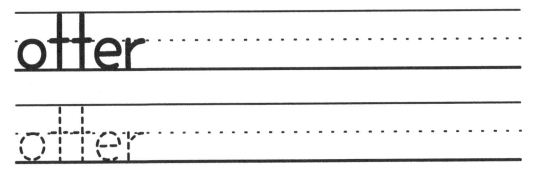

Scientific name: Lutrinae

I live: near water, almost everywhere on the globe!

I eat: fish and a variety of aquatic wildlife

I can live up to: 13 years old

Fun fact: Sea otters have very thick fur - about
1 million hairs per square inch!

Can you count how many hairs you have?!

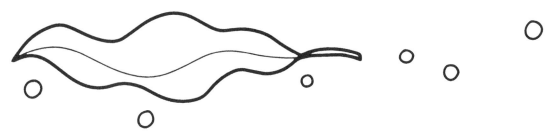

yak

Write the animal name below. Use your very best handwriting!

yak

yak

Scientific name: Bos grunniens

I live: in Central Asia

I eat: grasses

I can live up to: 20 years old

Fun fact: Yaks have long, wooly coats that keep them warm in freezing temperatures.

Does it get really cold where you live?!

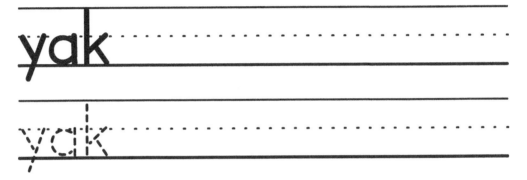

A very bear-y hello to the

bear

Write the animal name below. Use your very best handwriting!

bear

bear

Scientific name: Ursidae

I live: in a variety of habitats around the world

I eat: leaves, roots, berries, insects, fish & meat

I can live up to: 35 years old

Fun fact: Bears are large and incredibly strong!

How strong are YOU?! Let's see those muscles!

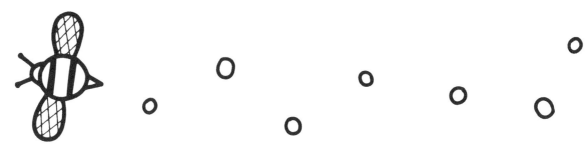

fennec fox

Write the animal name below. Use your very best handwriting!

fennec fox

fennec fox

Scientific name: Vulpes zerda

I live: in the desert

I eat: various rodents, bugs and eggs

I can live up to: 10 years old

Fun fact: Fennec foxes have ears that are

4 to 6 inches long!

Can you measure how big your ears are?!

kangaroo

Write the animal name below. Use your very best handwriting!

kangaroo

kangaroo

Scientific name: Macropodidae

I live: in Australia

I eat: grasses and plants

I can live up to: 12 years old

Fun fact: I can hop almost 30 feet in one single jump, but I can't walk backwards!

Can you imagine if you couldn't walk backwards?!

badger

Write the animal name below. Use your very best handwriting!

badger ....

badger

Scientific Name: Meles meles

I live: in prairies and plains

I eat: mice, rats, rabbits, frogs, & hedgehogs

I can live up to: 24 years old

Fun fact: I dig burrows and mazes of tunnels underground!

Do you want to dig a tunnel with me?!

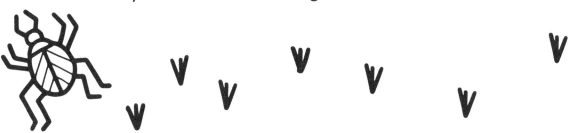

elephant

Write the animal name below. Use your very best handwriting!

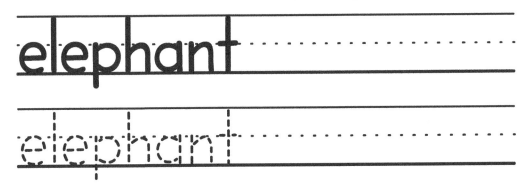

Scientific name: Loxodonta

I live: in Africa and Asia

I eat: tree bark, twigs, fruits, bushes, & grasses

I can live up to: 70 years

Fun fact: Elephants love spraying each other (and people) with water!

Would you like to be sprayed by an elephant?!

ostrich

Write the animal name below. Use your very best handwriting!

ostrich

ostrich

Scientific name: Struthio camelus

I live: in Africa

I eat: plants, lizards, insects, or small rodents

I can live up to: 40 years old

Fun fact: Ostriches are the largest bird in the WORLD, but they can't fly!

Can you believe there are birds that can't fly?!

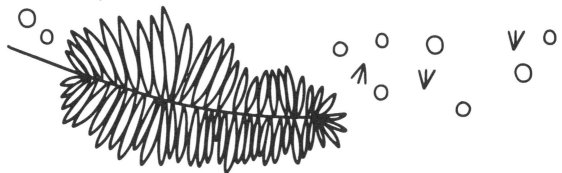

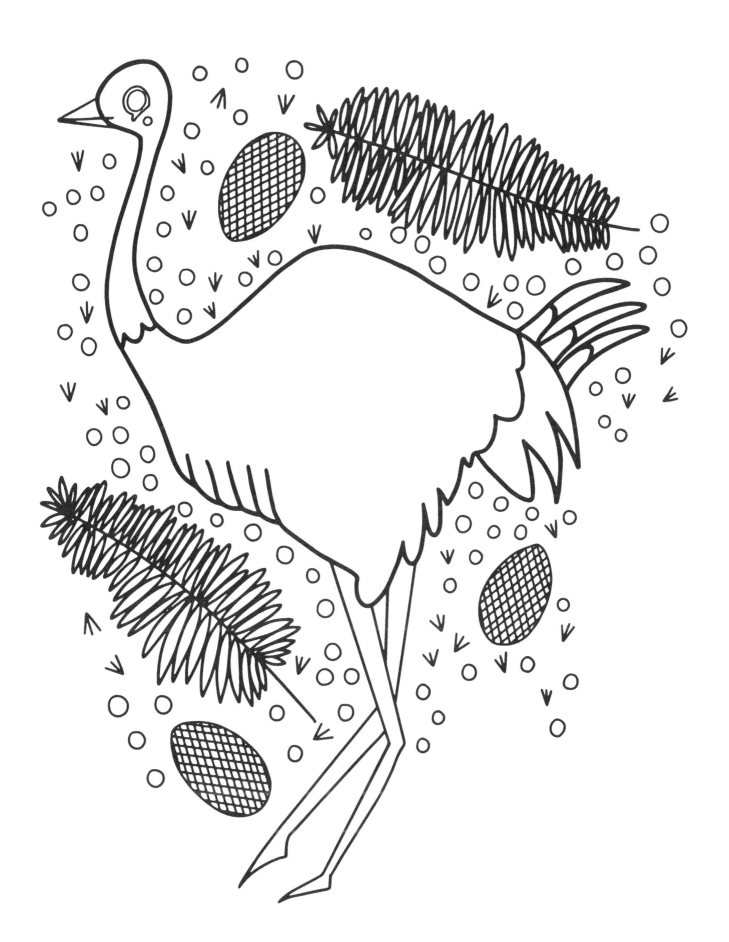

monkey

Write the animal name below. Use your very best handwriting!

monkey

monkey

Scientific name: Simiiformes catarrhini

I live: in tropical rainforests

I eat: leaves, flowers, nuts, fruits and insects

I can live up to: 20 years old

Fun fact: Monkeys have their own fingerprints, just like people!

What kind of monkeying around can you do?!

rabbit

Write the animal name below. Use your very best handwriting!

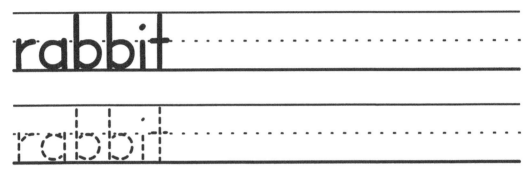

rabbit

rabbit

Scientific name: Oryctolagus cuniculus

I can: jump 2 feet vertically

I eat: grass, fruits and vegetables

I can live up to: 9 years old

Fun fact: Rabbits can have up to nine babies at a time!

How would you feel if you had 8 brothers and sisters?!

Let's slowly look at the

snail

Write the animal name below. Use your very best handwriting!

snail

snail

Scientific name: Gastropoda

I live: anywhere there is land

I eat: thick leaved plants, fruits, and veggies

I can live up to: 5 years old

Fun fact: Snails are so slow they only move half an inch per second!

See how slow you can walk! Go even slower!

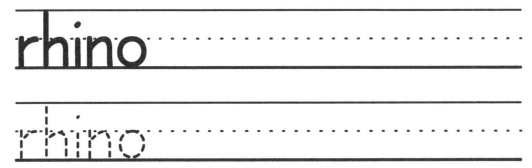

Let's stomp on over to the

rhino

Write the animal name below. Use your very best handwriting!

rhino

rhino

Scientific Name: Rhinocerotidae

I live: in Africa and Southern Asia

I eat: trees and bushes

I can live up to: 50 years old

Fun fact: Some rhinos can weigh over 7,700 lbs! That is more than a car!

How much do you weigh?! Compare that to a rhino!

goose

Write the animal name below. Use your very best handwriting!

goose

goose

Scientific name: Anserini

I live: in grassy areas near water

I eat: anything I can graze like seeds, stems, grass, and grain

I can live up to: 10 years

Fun fact: Geese fly together in the shape of a "v"!

How fun would it be to fly high like a goose?!

Dive down deep to meet the

whale

Write the animal name below. Use your very best handwriting!

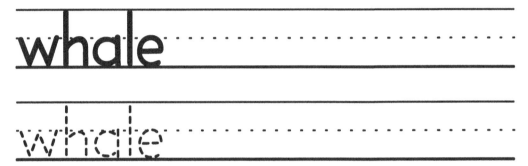

whale

whale

Scientific name: Cetecea

I live: in the ocean

I eat: fish, squid, octopus and other marine life

I can live up to: 70 years

Fun fact: The blue whale is so large, it's almost as long as 2 school buses!

Would you like to see the ocean through the eyes of a whale?!

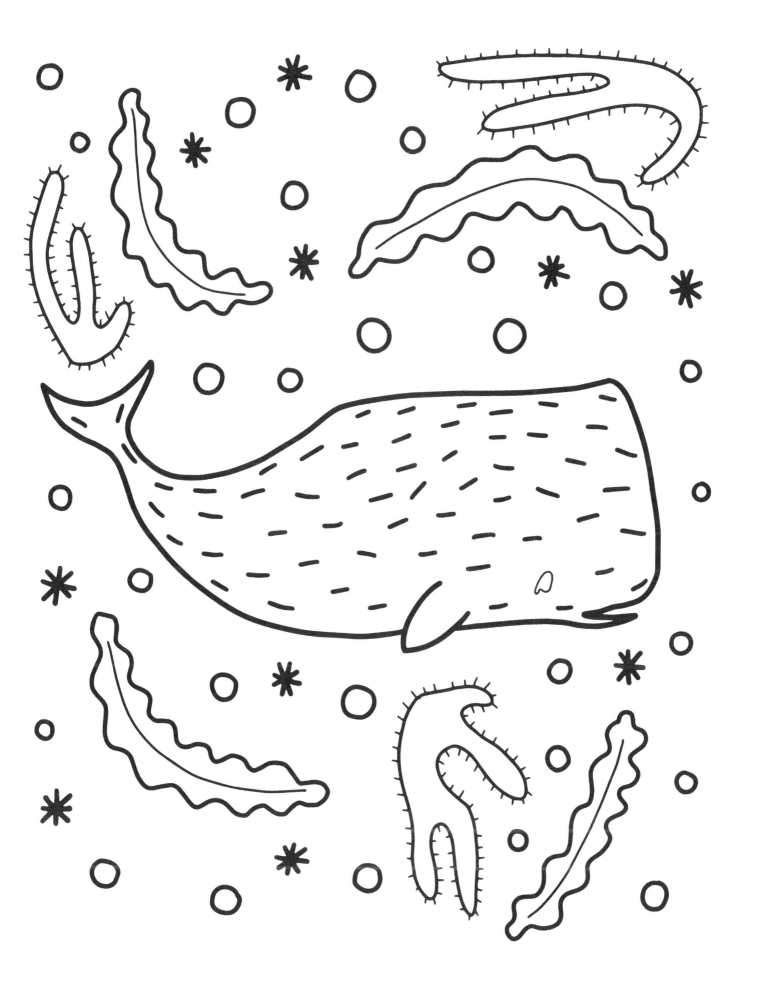

Take a peek at the

raccoon

Write the animal name below. Use your very best handwriting!

raccoon

raccoon

Scientific name: Procyon lotor

I live: in North America

I eat: insects, eggs, small mammals, fruit, berries, and garbage- yuck!

I can live up to: 3 years old

Fun fact: Raccoons have 5 fingers just like human hands!

Would you like to eat garbage for dinner?!

swan

Write the animal name below. Use your very best handwriting!

swan

swan

Scientific name: Cygnus

I live: near the water

I eat: aquatic vegetation, frogs, fish & worms

I can live up to: 30 years old

Fun fact: Swans can fly even though they
are very large birds!

Have you ever seen a huge bird fly in the sky?!

tiger

Write the animal name below. Use your very best handwriting!

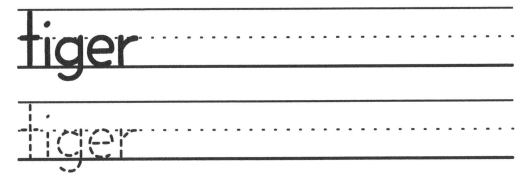

Scientific name: Panthera tigris

I am: an endangered species

I eat: other animals!

I can live up to: 15 years old

Fun fact: Tigers enjoy playing and swimming in the water!

Would you go swimming with a tiger?!

alligator

Write the animal name below. Use your very best handwriting!

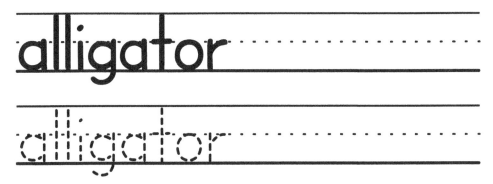

Scientific name: Alligator (same!)

I live: in swamps, marshes and lakes in the United States and China

I eat: mostly fish, turtles, birds & small animals

I can live up to: 50 years old

Fun fact: Alligators have been living on this Earth for millions of years!

How long have you been living on this Earth?!

squirrel

Write the animal name below. Use your very best handwriting!

squirrel

squirrel

Scientific name: Sciuridae

I live: wooded habitats all around the world

I eat: fruit, berries, nuts, bugs, fungi, eggs, seeds, and plants

I can live up to: 18 years old

Fun fact: Squirrels use their big bushy tail and twitch it to signal if they sense danger.

Would you like to have a big bushy tail?!

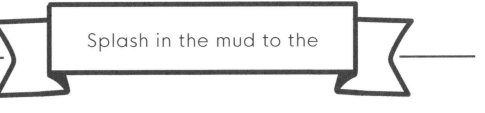

Splash in the mud to the

water buffalo

Write the animal name below. Use your very best handwriting!

Scientific name: Bubalus bubalis

I live: in the tropical forests of Asia

I eat: plants, herbs, and grass

I can live up to: 9 years old

Fun fact: Water Buffaloes have extra wide hooves that keep them from sinking in the mud.

Do you take mud baths like the water buffalo?!

toucan

Write the animal name below. Use your very best handwriting!

toucan

toucan

Scientific name: Ramphastidae

I live: in the rainforest of South & Central America

I eat: insects and fruits

I can live up to: 20 years old

Fun fact: Toucans are best known for their large, colorful bills!

How will you color your Toucan's bill?! Let's see!

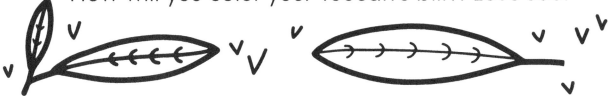

skunk

Write the animal name below. Use your very best handwriting!

skunk

skunk

Scientific name: Mephitis mephitis

I live: in North and South America

I eat: whatever I can find!

I can live up to: 3 years old

Fun fact: Some skunks do a handstand on their front paws when they spray!

Can you do a handstand like a skunk?!

giraffe

Write the animal name below. Use your very best handwriting!

giraffe

giraffe

Scientific name: Giraffa

I live: on the savannas in Africa

I eat: leaves and twigs of trees

I can live up to: 25 years

Fun fact: Giraffes are the tallest living animals!

How tall do you think you'll grow to be?!

seahorse

Write the animal name below. Use your very best handwriting!

seahorse

seahorse

Scientific name: Hippocampus

I live: in shallow tropical water

I eat: plankton and a variety of small fish & shrimp.

I have no teeth so I have to swallow my food whole!

I can live up to: 3 years old

Fun fact: Sea horses swim upright!

What foods would you eat if you didn't have teeth?!

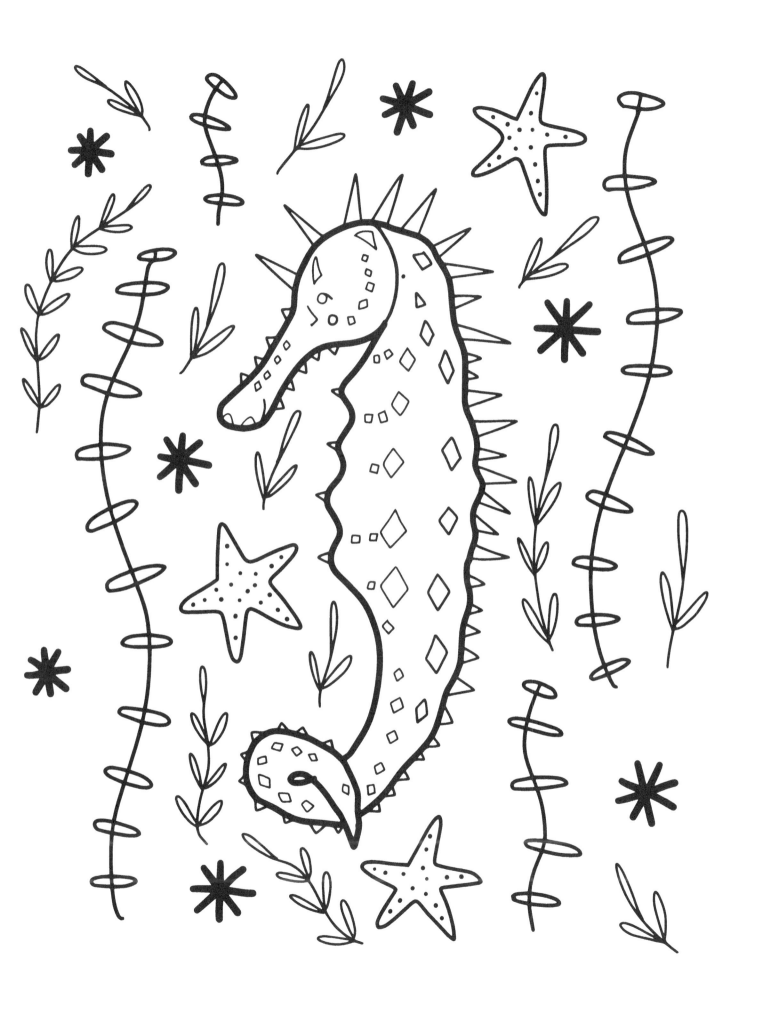

Take a look at the vibrant

flamingo

Write the animal name below. Use your very best handwriting!

flamingo

flamingo

Scientific name: Phoenicopterus ruber

I live: near lagoons or lakes

I eat: shrimp, algae and crustaceans

I can live up to: 30 years old

Fun fact: Flamingos are pink in color because of the food they eat!

Can you stand on one leg like a flamingo?!

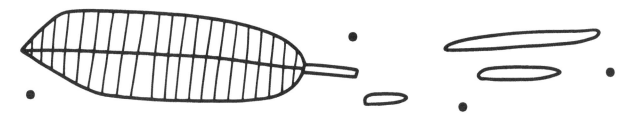

Try to see the speedy

gazelle

Write the animal name below. Use your very best handwriting!

gazelle

gazelle

Scientific name: Gazella

I live: in Africa and Asia

I eat: leaves, stems and grasses

I can live up to: 12 years old

Fun fact: Gazelles can run 40 miles per hour!

How many miles per hour can you run?!

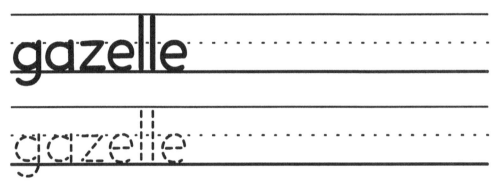

Let's mooooove on to the

COW

Write the animal name below. Use your very best handwriting!

COW

COW

Scientific name: Bos taurus

I live: in grasslands

I eat: grass, grains and hay

I can live up to: 22 years old

Fun fact: Cow's milk can be made into butter, yogurt and cheese!

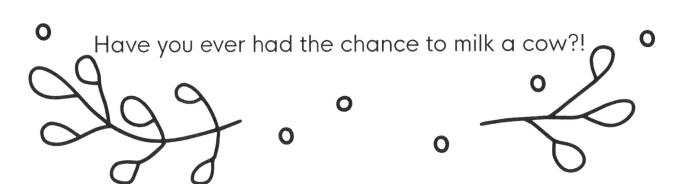

Have you ever had the chance to milk a cow?!

zebra

Write the animal name below. Use your very best handwriting!

zebra

zebra

Scientific name: Equus quagga

I live: in Africa

I eat: grass

I can live up to: 25 years

Fun fact: Every zebra has a unique pattern to their stripes!

Just like every zebra is unique, you are unique, too!

armadillo

Write the animal name below. Use your very best handwriting!

armadillo

armadillo

Scientific name: Dasypodidae

I live: in deserts, grasslands and rainforests

I eat: beetles and worms

I can live up to: 15 years old

Fun fact: Armadillos are covered in plates that look like a shell or armor that help to protect them!

Do you ever wear armor to protect yourself?!

Just look at the massive

buffalo

Write the animal name below. Use your very best handwriting!

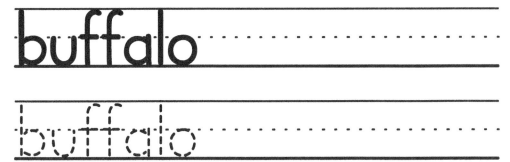

Scientific name: Bison bison

I live: on prairies and plains

I eat: grasses

I can live up to: 20 years old

Fun fact: A buffalo will roll in the dirt to shoo away flies that bite and help shed their fur.

Do you ever roll in the dirt like a buffalo?!

Let's look at the lovely

llama

Write the animal name below. Use your very best handwriting!

llama

llama

Scientific name: Lama glama

I live: all over South America, Australia, North America and Europe

I eat: different types of grass, grains, and hay

I can live up to: 20 years old

Fun fact: Llamas communicate by humming or moving their tails and ears!

Challenge: instead of talking today, just hum!

cat

Write the animal name below. Use your very best handwriting!

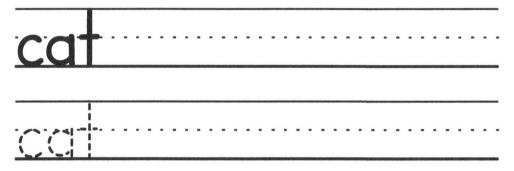

Scientific name: Felis catus

I can: jump about 5 times my height

I eat: mostly cooked meat in cat food!

I can live up to: 18 years old

Fun fact: A house cat is over 95% tiger- yikes!

Do you have a cat?! If so, color the picture like your cat!

Climb up a tree to see the

goat

Write the animal name below. Use your very best handwriting!

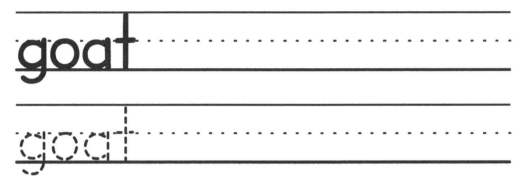

Scientific name: Capra aegagrus hircus

I live: in plains all around the world

I eat: grass, bushes, trees and grains

I can live up to: 18 years old

Fun fact: Goats are very good climbers and can even climb up trees!

Wouldn't it be fun to climb trees with a goat?!

octopus

Write the animal name below. Use your very best handwriting!

octopus

octopus

Scientific name: Octopoda

I live: in the ocean

I eat: crustaceans, clams, prawns and fish

I can live up to: 5 years old

Fun fact: Octopus have 3 hearts and are completely boneless!

Can you imagine not having any bones?!

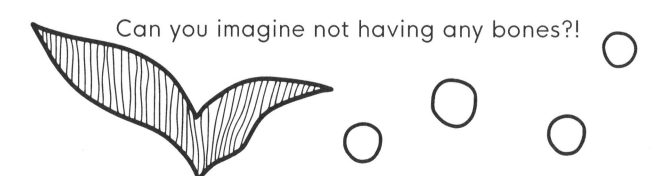

Better run fast to see the

leopard

Write the animal name below. Use your very best handwriting!

leopard

leopard

Scientific name: Panthera pardus

I eat: almost any animal that crosses my path!

I can: run up to 36 mph

I can live up to: 17 years old

Fun fact: Leopards purr when they feel happy!

The next time you're happy, purr like a leopard!

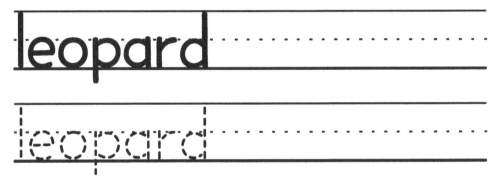

Peck on over to see the

chicken

Write the animal name below. Use your very best handwriting!

chicken

chicken

Scientific name: Gallus gallus domesticus

I live: on farms and in backyards

I eat: grains, fruits, vegetables, insects & mice

I can live up to: 10 years old

Fun fact: Like other pets, chickens can learn their names!

What do chickens lay? Color them on the next page!

It's time to welcome the

hedgehog

Write the animal name below. Use your very best handwriting!

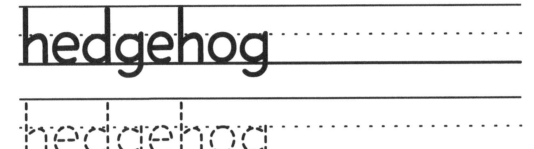

hedgehog

hedgehog

Scientific name: Erinaceinae

I live: in New Zealand, Africa, Asia, and Europe

I eat: whatever I can find! (bugs, frogs, eggs)

I can live up to: 5 years

Fun fact: Hedgehogs have around 5,000 spikes on their back!

Yikes! Spikes! Would you want to bump into a hedgehog?!

iguana

Write the animal name below. Use your very best handwriting!

iguana

iguana

Scientific name: Iguana iguana

I live: in rain forests

I eat: leaves off vines and trees

I can live up to: 8 years in the wild

Fun fact: Iguanas can grow up to 6 feet long!

What's the biggest iguana you have seen?!

Cuddle up to the

koala

Write the animal name below. Use your very best handwriting!

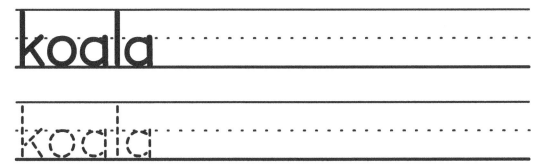

Scientific name: Phascolarctos cinereus

I live: in Australia

I eat: Eucalyptus leaves

I can live up to: 18 years old

Fun fact: Koalas sleep between 18-22 hours a day in order to digest their food!

Baby koalas cuddle up in their mama's pouch when they are first born!

owl

Write the animal name below. Use your very best handwriting!

owl

owl

Scientific name: Strigiformes

I live: on every continent except Antarctica

I eat: insects

I can live up to: 15 years old

Fun fact: Not every owl "hoots"! Some owls screech and hiss!

Did you know that owls are nocturnal, which means they are mainly active at night?!

fox

Write the animal name below. Use your very best handwriting!

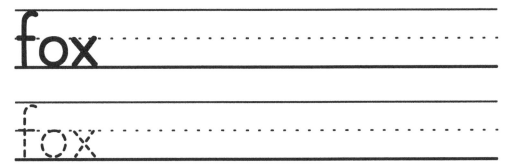

Scientific Name: Vulpes vulpes

I live: in burrows all over the world!

I eat: small animals, reptiles, birds, fruits, & bugs

I can live up to: 5 years old

Fun fact: I have whiskers on my face & legs!

They help me to navigate!

Would you like to have whiskers like a fox?!

horse

Write the animal name below. Use your very best handwriting!

horse

horse

Scientific name: Equus caballus

I can: run up to 55 mph

I eat: grass, hay, grains, fruit and vegetables

I can live up to: 25 years old

Fun fact: Horses can sleep when standing up!

Have YOU ever taken a nap standing up?!

panda

Write the animal name below. Use your very best handwriting!

panda

panda

Scientific name: Ailuropoda melanoleuca

I live: in central China

I eat: bamboo

I can live up to: 20 years old

Fun fact: Pandas can eat 12 hours per day!

What would you eat for 12 hours straight?!

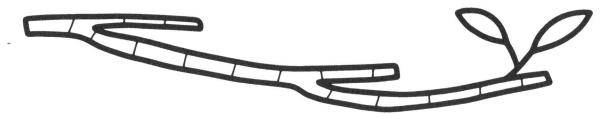

pig

Write the animal name below. Use your very best handwriting!

pig

pig

Scientific name: Sus scrofa domesticus

I live: in a wide variety of habitats with water and vegetation

I eat: whatever I can find on the ground including fruit, vegetables and bugs

I can live up to: 20 years old

Fun fact: Pigs use their snout (their nose) to locate food under the ground!

What is one of your favorite foods to smell?!

On land and sea, meet the

turtle

Write the animal name below. Use your very best handwriting!

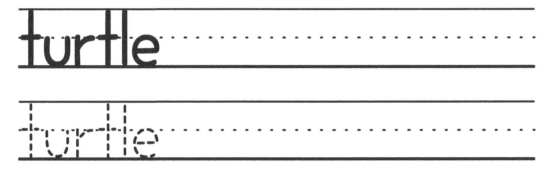

Scientific name: Testudines

I live: on every continent except Antarctica

I eat: worms, snails, insects, fruits, and flowers

I can live up to: 40 years (sea turtles live up to 80 years!)

Fun fact: Turtles have hard shells that they use as shields!

Make a shield today using things around the house!

vulture

Write the animal name below. Use your very best handwriting!

vulture

vulture

Scientific name: Aegypius Monachus

I live: on every continent except Australia and Antarctica

I eat: animals that have already died

I can live up to: 30 years old

Fun fact: Vultures have an excellent sense of smell to help them locate food.

Where would you go if you could fly?!

lion

Write the animal name below. Use your very best handwriting!

lion

lion

Scientific name: Panthera Leo

I live: in sub-Saharan Africa

I eat: meat!! Everything from birds to giraffes!

I can live up to: 14 years old

Fun fact: Lions live in groups called a "pride".

If you were a lion, who would be in your pride?!

Give a big howl-o to the

wolf

Write the animal name below. Use your very best handwriting!

wolf

wolf

Scientific name: Canis lupus

I can: run up to 37 mph

I eat: deer, elk, and moose

I can live up to: 8 years old

Fun fact: Wolves are known for their eerie howl, which is how they communicate.

Show someone your best HOWL like a wolf!

Made in the USA
Coppell, TX
20 September 2020